The Commandments of R&B Drumming Play-Along

A Play-Along Guide to Soul, Funk, and Hip-Hop

By

with **Russ Miller**

Cover photo by Heinz Kronberger.
Transcriptions and notation by Brian Mason.

Alfred Music Publishing Co., Inc.
16320 Roscoe Blvd., Suite 100
P.O. Box 10003
Van Nuys, CA 91410-0003
alfred.com

ISBN-10: 0-7390-5969-6 (Book & CD)
ISBN-13: 978-0-7390-5969-2 (Book & CD)

CONTENTS

"As a bassist, artist, and producer, what do you want to hear in a drummer?"
"Time, groove and feel—that's it!"

—Marcus Miller, Studio Bass Legend
Modern Drummer, June 1998

Acknowledgments and Credits

Thanks to God: The Source of All Things

First and foremost, I would humbly like to give thanks to God the Father, for the gift of life and music and for all the creative abilities and desires He has deposited in man; to the Holy Spirit for teaching me how to fulfill the dreams the Father placed in my heart, and for giving me the strength and courage necessary to pursue those visions to completion; to my Lord and Savior, Jesus Christ, I thank you for enduring the cross so that I would have eternal life and experience victory in this one.

Family

I wish to thank my wife, Renee, and my children, Jarod Christopher and Jordan Nicole, for blessing me and filling my life with unspeakable joy and inspiration. I live to serve you and thank God for you every day. I would like to thank my dearly departed mother, Maria, for being the absolute light of my life and the greatest mother a boy could have. She was a tremendous source of encouragement, inspiration, and love, and it was truly an honor to be her son. None of my success would have been possible without her. Thanks, Mother, for filling my heart with big dreams and high hopes, and for believing in me the way you did.

This book is dedicated to my wife and chldren, my mother, and to the memory of my friend Frank DaMatto, a man who picked me up when I was down and taught me the meaning of the word faith and how to believe and trust God, a man who made my life better because of his! I'll see you in Heaven, Frank! I also want to extend my deep gratitude to my sisters Patricia, Maria, and Lisa and my brothers Armando, Ricardo, and Robert. You have all played an integral role in what I have been able to achieve with my life. I also want to thank my in-laws Wil and Sandy Strong for their unbelievable faith and for being such a tremendous blessing through the years in every way!

Publisher

My sincere thanks to Ron Manus, John O'Reilly Jr., Rich Lackowski, Dave Black, Link Harnsberger, Ted Engelbart, Mark Burgess, Kate Westin, Michael Finkelstein, Antonio Ferranti, Karissa Read, Ann Miranda, Samantha Ordoñez, and the entire staff at Alfred Music Publishing for their hard work, support, and faith in all that I endeavor to do.

Partners

I wish to express my deepest gratitude to my partner Russ Miller for his dedication to excellence on every project we have collaborated on together, including this one! Quite obviously, this project would not be possible without him. I sincerely would like to thank the other partners I have been privileged to work with throughout the years: Lenny Kravitz, Jerry Hammack, Brian Mason, Amy Hagberg, and Daniel Glass. Your friendship, inspiration, and wisdom throughout our time together enriched my life so very much. You have made the fruit that I endeavored to bear much sweeter and have played pivotal roles in the success I have been fortunate enough to experience. THANK YOU!

Mentors

Much love, honor, and respect goes out to my early mentors who played key roles in shaping my formative years and helped me to become the person that I am today: Pearl Jones, Bill and Beverly Large, Kent Clinkingbeard, Donn Essig, and Ralph Johnson and Al McKay of Earth, Wind & Fire. Each of you has greatly blessed me, and I thank you from the bottom of my heart for the love that you so faithfully demonstrated to me!

Faithful Friends

In appreciation for blessing me with their gifts, talents, favor, faith, and friendship, a heartfelt thanks goes to Allen Rhodes, Carlo Krouzian, Tim Fogerty, Brian Mason, Amy Hagberg, Victoria Kemper, Anthony Albanese, Jackie Monaghan, Jusden Aumand, Robert Jolly, Kyle Prins, Eric and Shannon Rhodes, Dustin Ransom, Marty and Tracy Layton, Ray Brych, Glenn Noyes, Kenric Knecht, Dave and Joyce Meyer, Dr. Chris Norton, Dr. Cynthia Curtis, and all the staff at Belmont University in Nashville, Tennessee. I would also like to thank Compassion International and the Big Brothers Big Sisters of America organizations for allowing me the privilege of partnering with them in the great work they do around the world to change the lives of children.

Inspiration

I would like to extend my deepest love and appreciation to all the recording artists, drummers, authors and journalists referred to, mentioned, or quoted throughout this book for their inspiration and amazing contributions to the world of soul, funk, and hip-hop. My deepest thanks to each of the following drummers featured throughout the book: Bernard "Pretty" Purdie, Nat Kendrick, Joseph "Zigaboo" Modeliste, Richard "Pistol" Allen, John "Jabo" Starks, James Gadson, Freddie White, Earl Young, and Ricky Wellman. Each of you have inspired me personally and so many of us in the drumming community at large. We are grateful for your contribution to drumming and for your faithfulness in developing the gifts that God gave you and share with us!

Music Publisher and Industry

Thanks to the following organizations for their contribution to the advancement of drumming and education; I'm privileged to know and work with you and your staff: Belmont University, Berklee College of Music, Percussive Arts Society, National Association of Jazz Educators, The Rock 'n' Roll Hall of Fame, and NAMM (National Association of Music Merchants).

I would also like to acknowledge my appreciation to the following magazines for their support and friendship throughout my career—Thank you all!: *Modern Drummer, Drum!, Rhythm, Drum Head, Classic Drummer, Rhythm, Drummer, Todo Percussion, Bateria, Total, Batera and Percussao, Slagwerkkrant, Sticks, Drums and Percussion, Rhythm and Drums, Drum Club, Drums Etc., Batteur, Drum Scene,* and *Percussioni;* I also wish to thank Bernhard Castiglioni at drummerworld.com and all other drum publications throughout the world.

Zoro's Equipment

My sincere thanks to the following companies and their staff for their friendship, incredible and innovative equipment, and clinic support throughout the years: Drum Workshop Drums, Sabian Cymbals, Evans Drumheads, Vic Firth Sticks, Latin Percussion, Audix Microphones, SKB Cases, and Danmar Beaters. It's an honor to be associated with you and to represent you around the world. My thanks to each and every one of the people at those companies who dedicated themselves to excellence! You guys rock!

Zoro Clinic Support

Lastly, I would like to thank all of the drum shops, music stores, and music chains (especially Guitar Center and Sam Ash), drum schools, professors, music colleges, and festivals throughout the world that invited me to share my passion at clinics and educational events around the globe. It has been a privilege to spread the gospel of groove and the joy of drumming with those entrusted to you. I thank you sincerely for allowing me the opportunity to share my passion and my heart.

Literary Sources and Research Acknowledgments

All research done by Zoro. Additional sources include all liner notes from the recommended CDs and a plethora of books and articles on the history of rhythm and blues music.

Cover Art Credits and Special Thanks

Aretha Franklin *Amazing Grace* courtesy of Atlantic Records; James Brown *Think* courtesy of Universal; The Meters *Hey Pockey A-Way* courtesy of Sundazed Music; *Four Tops Anthology* courtesy of Universal; James Brown *Super Bad* courtesy of Universal; *Charles Wright & The Watts 103rd Street Rhythm Band* courtesy of Warner Bros.; Earth, Wind & Fire *All 'N All* courtesy of Columbia Records; MFSB *Love Is the Message* courtesy of Sony Music and Legacy/Rhythm & Soul; Chuck Brown & the Soul Searchers *Bustin' Loose* courtesy of Valley Vue Records; Guy *Guy* courtesy of MCA Records; Janet Jackson *The Velvet Rope* courtesy of Virgin Records.

Quote Credits and Special Thanks

Modern Drummer and *Rhythm* U.S. quotes were originally given courtesy of Ron Spagnardi, founder of Modern Drummer Publications. *The Great Drummers of R&B, Funk and Soul* quotes are courtesy of Jim Payne and Mel Bay Publications.

All photos used by permission.

CD Production Credits

This CD was produced and mixed by Russ Miller unless otherwise noted.
This CD was recorded at R.M.I. Productions, Sherman Oaks, CA by Russ Miller.

Special Thanks

I wish to give special props to my boys who made this music what it is: Russ Miller, Al McKay, Donn Wyatt, and Kevin Wyatt. It has been a blessing and an honor to work with all of you. To have such dear friends and great musicians be a part of my vision is a dream come true. You guys are simply the best and monsters in your own right. The level of musicianship exemplified on this CD would not be nearly what it is without your expertise, passion, and the extra love you put into it. I love you guys!

My gratitude also goes out to the rest of the talented musicians who gave of themselves to this project: Adam Jackson, Christine Miller, George Shelby, Jon Pappenbrook, and Mick Lane. Also, extra special thanks goes to Robby Robinson for his incredible musicianship, friendship, and help with his portion of the music.

Musician Credits for All Songs Except "Souledified," "Sho 'Nuff," and "The Funky Monk"

Produced and mixed by Russ Miller, Zoro, and Robby Robinson
Drums: Zoro
Percussion: Russ Miller
Guitar: Al McKay
Keyboards: Donn Wyatt
Bass: Kevin Wyatt
Vocals: Adam Jackson, Christine Miller
Trumpet: Jon Papenbrook
Sax: George Shelby
Trombone: Mick Lane
All drums played live by Zoro on the video set of this recording at
     The Complex in West Los Angeles, CA
All percussion played live during post-production at RMI Studios in Sherman Oaks, CA, by Russ Miller
No drum machine or programming was used for this recording.

Musician Credits for "Souledified," "Sho 'Nuff," and "The Funky Monk"

Drums: Zoro
Guitar: Fino "Skank Funk" Roverato
Keyboards: Robby Robinson
Bass: Rex "Tripoperous" Robinson
Sax: Tommy Alvarado
"Souledified," "Sho 'Nuff," and "The Funky Monk" written by Robby Robinson, Zoro,
     Fino Roverato, and Rex Robinson

A Special Note about the Recording of this Music

In order to recreate the original music featured on the enclosed CD in the most authentic manner possible and achieve the best possible recording, my partner Russ Miller and I decided to shoot the DVD a little differently than what is considered the norm for projects of this nature. The normal procedure for instructional DVDs has been to record the entire band live on the production set the day of the shoot, but because of the nature of this project and the goal of the subject matter, we found the traditional method to be a bit limiting and felt that it would not achieve the desired results. So Russ set on a rather difficult mission that involved a lot more time, hard work, and technical considerations.

In light of that, we decided to record all the music in advance of the DVD shoot. I played live with the entire rhythm section in the studio with a click track, then horns and vocals were added in post-production after the DVD shoot. Needless to say, this was a monstrous undertaking because we were approaching this recording like an album and not a DVD shoot.

Finally, on the day of the shoot, I had the complete arrangements laid out and a roughly mixed version of each tune to play along with. This way, we were able to strictly concentrate on re-recording the drums live that day.

Russ simply pulled the old drums out, and I played a new performance to the existing rhythm section tracks along to the click track. This worked out wonderfully and achieved some amazing sonic results. First of all, we had no bleed from other instruments, nor did we waste time on the set with all the possible room for error with 15 musicians recording all those songs at once. Also, had we not done it this way, every song would have had the same sound with little variance because we would not have had any control later to go in and make each song sound closer to the original recording.

Since the whole point of the DVD and this package was to show you the evolution of R&B music and drumming, we felt it was essential to capture the real sound and feel of each era as closely as we could, given our means, especially with regards to the recording of the actual music. So, we sincerely hope you enjoy the effort taken to make this a most enjoyable play along. My hat's off to Russ Miller for making all of this happen! Stay funky!

—Zoro

(Courtesy of Zoro)

Celebrating with my friend Russ Miller
Russ Miller has contributed greatly to my success as an author and educator through our joint efforts on the original Commandments of R&B Drumming book and DVD as well as this package. I am grateful for his friendship and dedication to excellence. Here we are at his house in Los Angeles for a New Year's Eve celebration. Thanks Russ for all you have done to bless my life!

How to Access the MP3 Play-Along Tracks on the Enhanced CD

Place the CD in your computer's CD-ROM drive.

Windows: Double-click on My Computer, then right-click on your CD drive icon and select Explore. Open "MP3" to view the MP3 files. Double-click on a file to view it immediately or save it to a folder on your hard drive to view later.

Mac: Double-click on the CD volume named "TnT Song Player" on your desktop. Open the "Play-Along Tracks" folder to view the MP3 files. Double-click on a file to view it immediately or save it to a folder on your hard drive to view later.

About the TnT Feature on the Enhanced CD

You can use the TnT software on your enhanced CD to change tempos, loop playback, and mute the drums for play-along. For complete instructions see the TnT ReadMe.pdf file on your enhanced CD.

Heroes: A Tribute to My Mentors

Behind any successful person is a team of individuals who helped to shape and mold that person into what they would eventually become. I would like to thank the following individuals for seeing the gold in me when I was only clay. For mining the diamond out of me when I was only a rock. For sowing into me when I was only a seed in the ground. These are the people who selflessly blessed my life with their love, friendship, encouragement, and faith in my abilities. Their investment in me allowed my life to flourish and thrive in a meaningful and purposeful way.

Without them, I would not be who I am today, nor would I have accomplished what I have been fortunate enough to do. I will be eternally grateful to God for placing each of them in my life's path. Thank you all so much for investing in me—you have my deepest love, gratitude, admiration, and respect.

My mother Maria, my sister Patricia, Pearl Jones, Bill and Beverly Large, Kent Clinkingbeard, and Ralph Johnson, and Al McKay of Earth, Wind & Fire. These are my heroes and, with the exception of my mother, all are still alive and I am honored to remain friends with them to this day!

Here I am at the beginning of my drumming journey back in 1979

With my mother Maria at the bull fights in Mexico City wearing my first official Zoro hat!

With my sister Patricia backstage at a Lenny Kravitz concert in New York City.

With Bill & Beverly Large, backstage at a concert I played with Frankie Valli & the Four Seasons.

With Pearl Jones, the first person who gave me a start in music.

With Kent Clinkingbeard, my first professional drum teacher.

My early mentor, drum teacher, and friend, Ralph Johnson of Earth, Wind & Fire.

Hanging with Al McKay after a show we played together.

About the Author

ZORO: A GROOVE FOR THE GENERATIONS

Zoro is the consummate definition of the rare man who marches to the beat of a different drum.

Zoro has sat on the drummer's throne commanding some of the most famous stages in the world of rock and R&B music. One of the funkiest drummers on the planet, Z has toured and recorded with Lenny Kravitz, Bobby Brown, Frankie Valli and the Four Seasons, The New Edition, Jody Watley, Philip Bailey of Earth, Wind & Fire, Vanessa Paradis, Sean Lennon, Lisa Marie Presley, Lincoln Brewster, Barlow Girl, and many others.

Throughout his career, he has consistently been voted No. 1 R&B Drummer and Clinician in the world by premier music industry publications such as *Modern Drummer*, *DRUM!*, and *Rhythm* magazines.

Often called the "Minister of Groove," Zoro authored the No. 1 award-winning and best-selling book and DVD package, *The Commandments of R&B Drumming*, which was awarded industry accolades as the ultimate lesson from the master.

With Daniel Glass, Z also co-authored another definitive work, *The Commandments of Early Rhythm and Blues Drumming*, which was released in 2008.

"Zoro wrote the book on dynamics, touch, control and groove," says *Modern Drummer* magazine. One of Z's most inspiring performances can be seen on the DVD titled *Modern Drummer Festival 2005* (Hudson Music).

Z is a sought-after player, motivational speaker, and clinician because he's real, relevant, and relatable, and connects with all generations. He has the heart of a true teacher and is motivated to serve and inspire his audience with all that he has.

Zoro is a kinetic bundle of human energy and enthusiasm. His heartbeat is in the groove itself, and his is "a groove for the generations."

To find out more about Zoro go to
www.zorothedrummer.com.

We all have a choice in life whether to build or destroy. For that reason, it's imperative to have a mission that motivates us, a positive inner driving force that gives us purpose. Invest your time, energy, and money in that purpose and in the pursuit of your dreams and goals by developing the talent you were given. Each of us is responsible for our own destiny; the choice is ours. Make the right one and choose a path of construction. Build towards your future with desire, determination, and drumming and let nothing negative stand between you and your dreams. Drugs are only a path for destruction, they cannot promote success; only practice, hard work, and persistence can do that.

—Zoro

Introduction

Welcome to my DVD play-along book and CD. It brings me great joy to see this long-time vision of mine come to fruition! My partner, Russ Miller, and I have gone to great lengths to bring you the best play-along package possible. An incredible amount of hard work, love, and passion went into this project for your benefit. I hope you enjoy playing along with this incredible music as much as we enjoyed making it. I have met a great many of you out on the road while touring, speaking, and doing clinics on the subject of my life-long passion, R&B drumming. This package comes to life as a direct result of the desire that many of you expressed to me for a play-along package that was truly authentic. So here it is, brothers and sisters. Dig in!

This play-along package chronologically documents the evolution of R&B drumming. It features 11 of the all-time funkiest tunes covering the most significant sub-genres of R&B music from the 1950s through the late 1990s. Styles include gospel, blues, New Orleans funk, Motown, soul, funk, go-go, new jack swing, and hip-hop, right on to the contemporary urban R&B grooves of today. There are also three bonus tracks in the style of these legendary R&B songs for you to play along with as well.

Original songs by R&B legends such as James Brown, The Meters, Aretha Franklin, Earth, Wind & Fire, and Janet Jackson are covered with true authenticity both in performance and in production. The CD features stellar performances by an all-star R&B band that includes legendary Earth, Wind & Fire guitarist Al McKay. Documentation for each song includes historical background information about the original recording and drummer, tips on approaching the music, rare photos, and album cover artwork. Also included are recommended listening guides to help you master each feel and a top-10 list of my favorite recordings for each featured drummer to inspire further study.

Along with the above is a chart for each song, complete with a transcription of the drum groove in each major section. This package clearly redefines the traditional play-along, and we hope it proves to be a useful and inspirational tool for mastering the concepts of groove drumming!

For a more in-depth view into my concepts and philosophies, please refer to the following issues and articles that have appeared in *Modern Drummer* magazine:

Dancing with Destruction, February 1997
Ask a Pro: Playing to a Click Track, October 1997
Maximizing Your Practice Time, April 1998
Zoro Feature Interview, March 1999
Gettin' on the Good Foot, May 1999
The Drummers of Motown, July 1999
Developing the Funky Hi-Hat Part 1, February 2000
Developing the Funky Hi-Hat Part 2, April 2000
Zoro/Lenny Kravitz Cover Story Feature Interview, September 2004

Drum Key

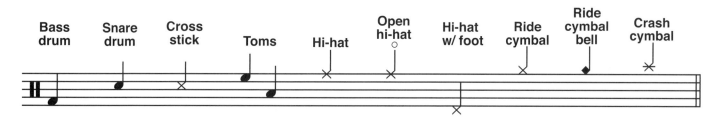

OLD LANDMARK
TWO-BEAT GOSPEL FEEL

Original Recording Profile

Recording Artist: Aretha Franklin
Producers: Jerry Wexler, Arif Mardin, and Aretha Franklin
Drummer: Bernard Purdie
Original Album: *Amazing Grace*
Record Label: Atlantic Records
Recording Date: January 14, 1972
Recorded live at New Temple Missionary Baptist Church in
    Los Angeles, CA

Historical Overview

This is a classic gospel song that has been covered by many artists. The particular version that we based the arrangement on was sung by the queen of soul herself, the great Aretha Franklin. It is from her seminal 1972 album titled *Amazing Grace*, which featured an amazing gospel choir and live orchestra. You may have heard this song if you've seen the movie *The Blues Brothers* starring Dan Aykroyd and John Belushi. James Brown played a Baptist minister and sang this song in the highly uplifting church scene. If this song doesn't immediately inspire you to start clapping on beats 2 and 4 then you may want to check your pulse because you are probably dead! If you can't find 2 and 4, you may want to reconsider pursuing a career as a drummer.

Approaching the Music

This song is based on a fast two-beat gospel swing feel. It's not uncommon, in the more old-school traditional gospel music, to hear the tambourine louder in the mix than the drums. This is especially true with regards to the original recording of this song. In fact, you can't hear the drums very well on this live recording, but you can feel them for sure. However, based on the style of music, there are only a few ways to approach playing a two-beat gospel song at this tempo. Listen closely to how the tambourine plays a variety of swung rhythms. This has a direct influence on the way I play my hi-hat and the bell of the ride cymbal on this song. Basically, it's similar to a jazz swing ride pattern with a steady R&B backbeat.

Recommended Recordings to Help Master This Feel

The Gospel Box (1999, Rhino Records)
Aretha Franklin's *Amazing Grace: The Complete Recording* (1999, Rhino Records)
Jubilation! Great Gospel Performances Vol. 1–3 (1992, Rhino Records)

---

10 Classic Bernard "Pretty" Purdie Tracks

1. "Rock Steady" by Aretha Franklin, 1971
2. "Home at Last" by Steely Dan, 1978
3. "Until You Come Back to Me (That's What I'm Gonna Do)" by Aretha Franklin, 1973
4. "Kid Charlemagne" by Steely Dan, 1976
5. "Babylon Sisters" by Steely Dan, 1980
6. "Deacon Blues" by Steely Dan, 1978
7. "The Fez" by Steely Dan, 1976
8. "Day Dreaming" by Aretha Franklin, 1972
9. "Green Earrings" by Steely Dan, 1976
10. "Memphis Soul Stew" by King Curtis from *Live at the Fillmore West*, 1971

(Courtesy of Bernard Purdie)

Bernard "Pretty" Purdie

The master of the groove, Bernard "Pretty" Purdie is one of the most recorded drummers of all time and most definitely one of the most groove oriented drummers to hit planet earth! This guy just keeps getting better. He plays with such intention, such depth of thought, and such joy of spirit. We are lucky to have so many great recordings he has given us. He is truly one of the most prolific players of our time.

(Courtesy of Zoro collection)

I have had the pleasure of playing with Bernard on many occasions, and it's always a privilege and honor as well as a great lesson. Here are a few photos of us hanging at various events throughout the years! The last photo ain't nothing but a groove and represents four generations of drummers dedicated to the pocket: Bernard Purdie, myself, and James Brown drummers Clyde Stubblefield and John "Jabo" Starks. It helps to be surrounded by the giants of groove!

Insight from the Masters

"He (the drummer) is the backbone of the band. If you take care of that job then you can do anything you want. Your job is to hold the band together. Your job is to support everybody in that band. It's your job to give the band what they want, when they need it. And in return, they'll give you what you need. But, you've got to give it to them first. Always, that's your role."

—Bernard Purdie
Modern Drummer, May/June 1979

"Some jazz drummers look down on rock 'n' roll because they don't know it. They can't interpret it, so they can't play it. They can't play it, so they don't like it. Rock 'n' roll has simplicity. Jazz is sometimes busy, and it's always easier to play busy. When you play busy, you can hide your mistakes, and the more you play, the more mistakes you'll make. That's why it's so hard to groove. When you're grooving, you don't have to play anything but 2 and 4, but when you miss, it sticks out like a sore thumb. It's harder to play rock and R&B than anything else, because it is so simple."

—Bernard Purdie
Modern Drummer, November 1985

OLD LANDMARK

Composed by
A.M. BRUNNER

MAIN GROOVE

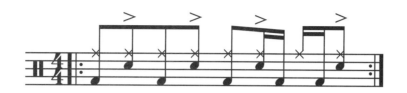

MAIN GROOVE VARIATIONS

BREAKDOWN VARIATIONS

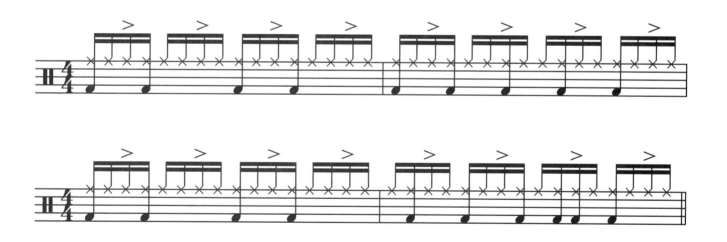

FILL IDEA

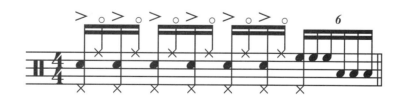

THINK
QUASI-BLUES SHUFFLE FEEL

Original Recording Profile

Recording Artist: James Brown
Producer: Unknown
Drummer: Nat Kendrick
Originally Released May 1960 as a Federal single
Appears on the CD re-issue *Think*,
    1996 Polygram Records, Inc.
Recording Date: February 20, 1960
Recorded at United Studios, Hollywood, CA

Historical Overview

This is a classic blues song that has been covered by many artists. Some of the other versions that I strongly recommend checking out include James Brown's, featuring John "Jabo" Starks on drums, as opposed to the James Brown arrangement here, which features drummer Nat Kendrick. James Brown has two versions of this same song, which was not uncommon during this period.

Approaching the Music

There are so many different types of shuffles and ways to approach them that one could dedicate themselves solely to that subject. In fact, someone has! For a comprehensive and in-depth look at this style and many other shuffles, please pick up a copy of *The Commandments of Early Rhythm and Blues Drumming* (2008, Alfred Music Publishing). This book was an 8-year collaboration between Daniel Glass and me and it's a monstrous and intensely thorough study on the subject. This song features a deceivingly complex shuffle that few drummers play well—in fact, it's almost becoming somewhat of a lost art these days. It was a feel that was quite common in the '40s, '50s and '60s era of rhythm and blues but is rarely heard today in an authentic manner.

The feel cannot accurately be written out because its true pulse lies somewhere in that sneaky place between straight eighths and the dotted eighth and sixteenth feel commonly associated with most regular shuffles. The key is to straighten out the dotted eighth and sixteenth feel on the hi-hat and bring it a little closer to the straight eighth feel, but not all the way; it has to be pushed in that direction ever so slightly.

The left hand has just a little bit more swing to it than the right. This is an incredible feel to play once you master it, but it takes quite a while to get a feeling for it. Nat Kendrick, who was from New York, was an absolute master of this feel! He plays this groove many times in a variety of ways on James Brown's double-CD set titled, *Roots of the Revolution*, a wise investment if there ever was one. Playing along with those recordings is simply the only way to get a true understanding of this feel. There are quite a few songs that perfectly depict this exact feel that can be found on this compilation.

Recommended Recordings to Help Master This Feel

James Brown's *Roots of the Revolution* (1989, Polygram)
Earl Palmer's *Backbeat: The World's Greatest Rock N' Roll Drummer* (1999, Ace Records), a 2-CD compilation
    of Earl's best work with Little Richard, Fats Domino, and a host of others!

10 Classic Nat Kendrick Tracks

1. "Good God Lovin'" by James Brown, 1959
2. "I'll Go Crazy" by James Brown, 1959
3. "Shout & Shimmy" by James Brown, 1961
4. "Maybe the Last Time" by James Brown, 1964
5. "Bewildered" by James Brown, 1960
6. "(Do The) Mashed Potatoes, Pt. 1" by James Brown, 1960
7. "Baby, You're Right" by James Brown, 1960
8. "Lost Someone" by James Brown, 1961
9. "Devil's Den" by James Brown, 1963
10. "Mashed Potatoes" by Nat Kendrick & The Swans, 1960

Nat Kendrick
Nat Kendrick is one of the most unknown groove drummers in history. Here he is in a publicity shot from the early 1960s.
Check out his work on the earlier James Brown recordings of the late '50s and early '60s. The man could shuffle his brains out and had a most prolific swing to his playing. A true servant of the groove if ever there was one!

Insight from the Masters

"You can't play blues by the paper. Blues is a feeling. There's no way in the world that you can put your feeling into no sheet music and say 'this is the way it's supposed to be played,' because it's not going to be coming out right...you can't play dynamics if you're playing too loud. You have no way to go up because you're already up...A drummer never gets out front. If you're playing in a band, the drummer stays behind everybody. Just like if you're in the Army, you've got somebody to back you up all the time.

"The scouts go out in the front. Well they've got to have some rear guard. The rear guard is your drummer. When the rear guard gets up front, that fouls up the whole thing. You get back there and you kick! If you're a good drummer you should always be respected and recognized. He has one of the hardest jobs in the band because he's got to keep everybody together; to pull everything together to tighten it up. Then push it out there so it sounds nice."

—Fred Below, Chess Records Blues Studio Legend
Modern Drummer, September 1983

A studio pioneer and one of the fathers of blues drumming, Fred Below.

THINK

Composed by
PAULING LOWMAN

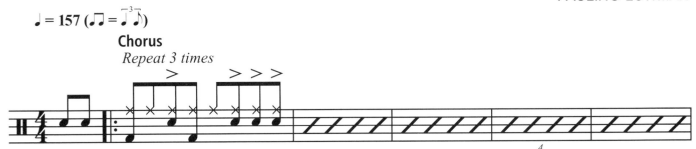

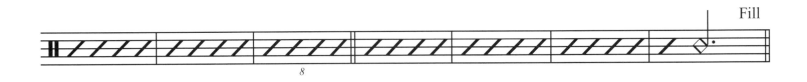

MAIN GROOVE

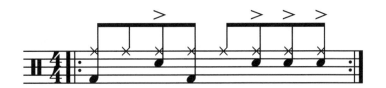

MAIN GROOVE VARIATIONS

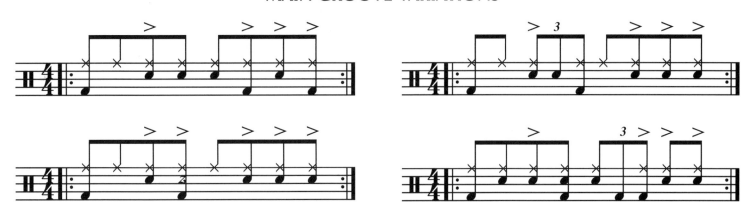

UNISON SHUFFLE EXERCISES

HEY POCKY A-WAY
NEW ORLEANS SECOND LINE FEEL

Original Recording Profile

Recording Artist: The Meters
Producer: Allen Toussaint
Drummer: Joseph "Zigaboo" Modeliste
Original Album: *Rejuvenation*
Record Label: Warner Brothers/Reprise
Recording Date: 1974

Historical Overview

The second line groove originated in New Orleans and has a very deep historical significance and cultural purpose. The second line feel began with people who would gather along and behind the band during parades and funerals in New Orleans. According to legendary drummer Earl Palmer, "They were just looking for any excuse to party. These folks would dance or bang on just about anything they could find that would make a percussive sound. These impromptu percussionists and dancers were dubbed the 'second line,' describing their position in the procession. This is what we have come to know as the second line beat."

Eventually, the strutters and dancers in the second line began to precede the brass and percussion sections of the band—acting in a fashion similar to drum majors in classic marching bands who accent and personify the pulse. The band would consist of trumpets, trombones, and a marching snare drummer and bass drum. This was a funeral procession N'awlins style.

The second line has since become one of the most recognizable characteristics of New Orleans culture. Whether for mourning or celebrating, the second line is a tradition that represents the heart and soul of the Crescent City. No doubt this particular rhythm evolved from the many rhythms that found their way to the New Orleans region through immigrants from as far away as the West Indies, Africa, and Europe.

Approaching the Music

Much like the previous James Brown tune, "Think," this particular groove also has a feel that lies in that mystery zone between straight and swung feels. You will find that it goes back and forth between straight eighths and the dotted eighth and sixteenth feel. It's kind of like a shuffle, but it really isn't exactly your standard blues shuffle. It's really its own, thing much like a lot of the music that has come out of the New Orleans region. It's a hybrid mixture of all its influences, played in a unique way that is truly *down home*.

Technically speaking, I approach playing this feel with a right hand lead on the snare, then with a left hand lead, then finally alternating left and right hand stickings while maintaining the necessary accents. I also practice this traditional second line rhythm doing unison patterns with both hands. Practicing all these possible variations lends me greater control over the rhythm and gives me more options and flexibility when it comes to performing it.

I like to intermittently incorporate buzz strokes with both the left and right hands, ruffs, and five stroke rolls. I also employ the use of the sidestick and a variety of finger ghost-note-oriented patterns. For a clear demonstration of this, please pick up my DVD that this play-along book is based on, *The Commandments of R&B Drumming: A Comprehensive Guide to Soul, Funk, and Hip-Hop.*

If you ever are really interested in seeing how many ways a snare drum can be played then I urge you to delve deeper into New Orleans drumming. I also like to practice very syncopated bass drum rhythms that lock in with the snare line. One great exercise to get your kick drum really together is to practice playing the second line snare drum part solely on your bass drum, with accents and all.

This is really a great challenge because drummers seldom work on accenting patterns on the bass drum alone. I have found this to be a great concept for developing seriously syncopated bass drum control. It gives me a lot of non-traditional phrasing options. The second line feel is one of the greatest feels we have as drummers, simply because it is so funky!

Recommended Recordings to Help Master This Feel

Funkify Your Life: The Meters Anthology (1995, Rhino)
The Neville Brothers' *Live on Planet Earth* (1994, A&M)
Dr. John's *In the Right Place* (1973, Atco)
New Orleans and Second Line Drumming DVD (2004, Alfred Music Publishing), Featuring Earl Palmer, Herlin Riley, Johnny Vidacovich, and Herman Ernest
Second Line: 100 Years of New Orleans Drumming by Antoon Aukes (2000, C.L. Barnhouse)

10 Classic Joseph "Zigaboo" Modeliste Tracks

1. "Chicken Strut" by The Meters, 1970
2. "Cissy Strut" by The Meters, 1969
3. "Fire on the Bayou" by The Meters, 1975
4. "People Say" by The Meters, 1974
5. "Right Place, Wrong Time" by Dr. John, 1973
6. "Funky Miracle" by The Meters, 1969
7. "Look-Ka-Py-Py" by The Meters, 1969
8. "Cabbage Alley" by The Meters, 1972
9. "Sophisticated Cissy" by The Meters, 1969
10. "Africa" by The Meters, 1974

(Courtesy of Joseph "Zigaboo" Modeliste collection)

Joseph "Zigaboo" Modeliste
One of the most original and inimitable drummers of our time: the ever-so-funky Joseph "Zigaboo" Modeliste of The Meters. He is revered by many as one of the drumming greats of R&B.

(Courtesy of Zoro collection)

The Zzzzz brothers: Zoro and Zig hanging at the NAMM (National Association of Music Merchants) show in Anaheim, California, in 1999. This shot was taken of Zig and me at the Sabian booth as we were talking about all the great grooves of R&B and how much we both love playing Sabian cymbals! Zig is the master of that loose, slimy, slinky, slanky, winky dinky dog kinda funk!

Insight from the Masters

"How well you play everything else doesn't mean anything if it's not in time. Consequently, I found that to be very true, and any time I have the occasion to do any kind of clinic or seminar that is the first thing I stress to the young drummers. If you are not playing that instrument in time, you are not playing that instrument."…"Make the rest of the guys know that you're responsible for the time. You're going to catch hell for it when it's bad and you seldom get the glory when it's good. Somehow establish a rapport with them that if they all play the time you're playing, if it's good and consistent, then you'll all be in time. You have to have a little bit of a take-over attitude without being overbearing, for the good of the time feel. You can't all be an individual leader and in that particular instance, you're the leader, in that section."

—Earl Palmer, Studio Legend
Modern Drummer, May 1983

"It's laid back, but not too laid back. And it's in the pocket. It's not a whole lot of technical stuff happening. It's feel, man. It's feel.

—Herman Ernest, New Orleans R&B Great
Modern Drummer, October 1990

HEY POCKY A-WAY

Composed by
LEO NOCENTELLI, ARTHUR
NEVILLE, JOSEPH MODELISTE,
and GEORGE JOSEPH PORTER

MAIN GROOVE

MAIN GROOVE VARIATIONS

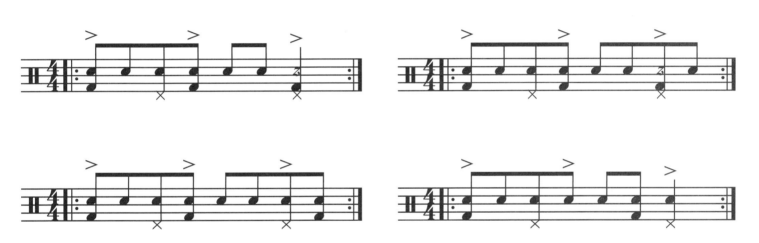

BRIDGE GROOVES

STANDING IN THE SHADOWS OF LOVE

$\frac{4}{4}$ MOTOWN FEEL

Original Recording Profile

Recording Artist: The Four Tops
Producers: Brian Holland and Lamont Dozier
Drummer: Richard "Pistol" Allen
Original Album: Released as a single on November 2, 1966
 on Motown's subsidiary label, Gordy
Record Label: Motown
Recording Date: 1966
Recorded at Hitsville Studios, Detroit, MI

Historical Overview

This particular groove started showing up on the charts as early as 1965 with the Four Tops classics "I Can't Help Myself (Sugar Pie Honey Bunch)" and "It's the Same Old Song." It was known as the "Motown beat" and was played most frequently by Benny Benjamin, Pistol Allen, and Uriel Jones, the three staff drummers at Motown between 1959–1972, although Pistol was the one who played this groove the most. Part of the magic of this groove was undoubtedly the bass lines of the master, James Jamerson.

It was the interplay between the bass line and the bass drum that was responsible for the motion this groove created. It was not uncommon for one of the drummers to be playing the main part of the groove while another would do the fills. This way they could keep that quarter-note pulse pumping all the way through the tune. Motown was very creative when it came to recording drum tracks.

Approaching the Music

The emphasis of this groove is that consistent quarter-note pulse played on the snare drum against the steady eighth notes on the hi-hat. Motown's legendary Pistol Allen played this groove for me in person once and it was absolutely magnificent. One of the keys to mastering this feel is to play it very light. They didn't pound the heck out of the snare as we so often do today. It was light and fluffy, floaty and airy-like, while still driving the pulse!

Recommended Recordings to Help Master This Feel

The Four Tops Anthology (1989, Polygram)
Hitsville USA: The Motown Singles Collection 1959–1971 (1989, Polygram)
Standing in the Shadows of Motown documentary DVD (2002, Artisan)

---

10 Classic Richard "Pistol" Allen Tracks

1. "(Love is Like a) Heatwave" by Martha and the Vandellas, 1963
2. "Baby Love" by The Supremes, 1964
3. "The Way You Do the Things You Do" by The Temptations, 1964
4. "I Can't Help Myself (Sugar Pie Honey Bunch)" by The Four Tops, 1965
5. "It's the Same Old Song" by The Four Tops, 1965
6. "How Sweet It Is (to Be Loved by You)" by Marvin Gaye, 1965
7. "Reach Out I'll Be There" by The Four Tops, 1966
8. "(Your Love Keeps Lifting Me) Higher and Higher" by Jackie Wilson, 1967
9. "Uptight (Everything's Alright)" by Stevie Wonder, 1966
10. "Jimmy Mack" by Martha and The Vandellas, 1967

(Courtesy of Richard "Pistol" Allen)

Richard "Pistol" Allen

Looking sharp and funky in this photo, Pistol was one of the sweetest cats in the business and a genuinely great man who is sorely missed! Every time I went to Detroit to do anything he would show up to support me. He was a one-of-a-kind man.

(Courtesy of Zoro collection)

The Motown groove master, Pistol Allen, and me hanging in my hotel room after one of my concerts with Frankie Valli & the Fours Seasons. We stayed up all night and just talked music, history, and life and it was awesome. This shot was taken in Detroit, Michigan, in 1997.

(Photo courtesy of Zoro collection.)

This is Pistol on my drumset at my soundcheck in Detroit. He played the beat to the classic Martha Reeves and the Vandellas song, "(Love Is Like a) Heatwave," and the entire band, which had just left the stage moments before, made an immediate U-turn because they knew something special just happened on stage. It was an unforgettable moment to hear him play because he had a sound that we all recognized from tons of Motown hit records he played on. What a thrill it was!

Here I am hanging out with my favorite Motown group, The Four Tops, after a show we did together in Las Vegas. The original line-up remained for 40 years, which is a near-impossible accomplishment in the music industry. For a deeper listen to their catalog of hits, pick up any of The Four Tops anthology packages. They had a great sound and Pistol Allen played on many of their hits.

(Courtesy of Zoro collection)

Insight from the Masters

"With today's musicians, everybody wants to be a star. Nobody just wants to play their parts like we did at Motown. If there was something magical that made that music sound good, it was the fact that everybody played a part. There's no musicality in just playing hard all the time. There's nothing to draw you in and make you listen."

—Pistol Allen
Modern Drummer, July 1999

STANDING IN THE SHADOWS OF LOVE

Composed by
EDWARD HOLLAND JR., LAMOND DOZIER,

MAIN GROOVE

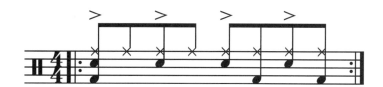

MAIN GROOVE VARIATIONS

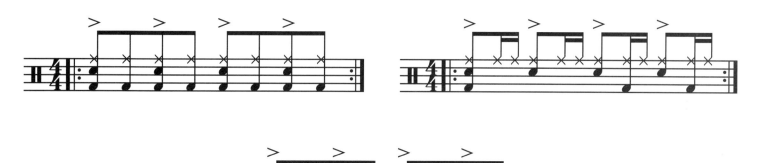

PRE-CHORUS GROOVE

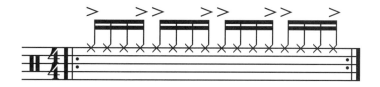

PISTOL ALLEN FILL

SUPER BAD
SYNCOPATED EIGHTH NOTE FEEL

Original Recording Profile

Recording Artist: James Brown
Producer: James Brown
Drummer: John "Jabo" Starks
Original Album: *Super Bad*
Record Label: King
Recording Date: June 30, 1970
Recorded at Starday-King Studios, Nashville, TN

Historical Overview

This is one of the funkiest tunes I have ever heard and a milestone groove that assured a place for John "Jabo" Starks in the annals of funk history. What makes this groove truly unique is the fact that it's one of the only tunes I can think of where the snare drum is actually played on beat 1. According to Jabo himself, on his *Soul of the Funky Drummers* DVD (1999, Rittor Music), this groove was inspired by a famous tap dance rhythm that he patterned the beat after.

Approaching the Music

In almost all genres of R&B music, playing the snare on beat 1 is rare. From the get go on this tune, the snare on beat 1 lines up with the horn stabs. Pay close attention to Jabo's ride work on the original record. He is the master of playing funky syncopated rhythms on the bell of the ride while never forsaking the groove. This entire drum beat is about orchestration. Every rhythm Jabo plays complements the arrangement and brings all the parts together in a most musical manner.

Once again, like many R&B drummers from his era, his approach is real light and sensitive because he was coming from a swing background. Jabo got schooled on all of this during his tenure with blues legend Bobby "Blue" Bland, with whom he played before James Brown. If there is one misconception about the drumming of James Brown (and R&B music in general from this time period), it's the assumption that they were slammin' the heck out of the drums with all their might. They played with real sensitivity and dynamic control. That's part of the secret to the sound and a skill that takes serious control and years to develop. Playing soft but with intensity and articulate authority is the sign of a true master.

Recommended Recordings to Help Master This Feel

James Brown's *Star Time* Box Set (1991, Polygram)
The Soul of the Funky Drummers DVD (1999, Rittor Music/Hal Leonard Corporation)

10 Classic John "Jabo" Starks Tracks

1. "Turn On Your Lovelight" by Bobby "Blue" Bland, 1961
2. "Licking Stick-Licking Stick" by James Brown, 1968
3. "Get Up (I Feel Like Being a Sex Machine)" by James Brown, 1970
4. "Make It Funky" by James Brown, 1971
5. "Talking Loud and Saying Nothing" by James Brown, 1972
6. "Doing It to Death (Funky Good Time)" by Fred Wesley and The JB's, 1973
7. "The Payback" by James Brown, 1974
8. "I Pity the Fool" by Bobby "Blue" Bland, 1961
9. "Stormy Monday Blues" by Bobby "Blue" Bland, 1962
10. "Driving Wheel" by Little Junior Walker, 1961

(Courtesy of Zoro collection)

The Vic Firth drumstick company's slogan is "the perfect pair," and here I am sandwiched between the perfect pair of two of the funkiest drummers God ever created: James Brown's emissaries of groove and pioneers of the funk beat, Clyde Stubblefield and John "Jabo" Starks, at the Vic Firth booth at the NAMM show in Los Angeles back in the 1990s. It sure seems like all the funky cats love playing Vic Firth! Jabo is one of the most gentle, yet relentless, groovers on the planet as well as a true tender-hearted loving man. He has a musical sensitivity that few can match and an attitude of grace and humility I have rarely seen.

Hanging with Motown drumming legend Pistol Allen and James Brown drummers Clyde Stubblefield and John "Jabo" Starks at the NAMM show in Los Angeles. This was a rare gathering of my absolute favorite drummers and people on the planet. These are the encounters that will live on in my heart forever!

(Courtesy of Zoro collection)

Insight from the Masters

"I'm not there to say I'm the world's greatest. I'm there to make the music happen. As a drummer you are the heartbeat of the group, you pump energy to all the instruments that are there. If you stop pumping, it's going to be dead. I think I was one of the first drummers who worked for James Brown who tried to accent his dance moves while keeping the groove."

—John "Jabo" Starks
Modern Drummer, September 1999

"I used to play with the metronome for at least six minutes straight. I'm not going to let you pull me and I'm not going with you. If you say the tempo is here, then it'll be here. When you finish what you're doing and get back, it'll be right here."

—John "Jabo" Starks
The Great Drummers of R&B, Funk & Soul by Jim Payne (Mel Bay Publications)

SUPER BAD

Composed by
JAMES BROWN

VERSE GROOVE

VERSE GROOVE VARIATIONS

BRIDGE GROOVE

BRIDGE GROOVE VARIATION

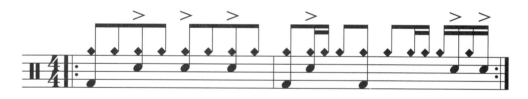

FILL

LOVE LAND
ONE-HANDED SIXTEENTH NOTE FEEL

Original Recording Profile

Recording Artist: Charles Wright & the Watts 103rd Street
   Rhythm Band
Producers: Charles Wright and the Watts 103rd Street Rhythm Band
   (Bill Cannon, Melvin Dunlap, Gabe Flemings, James Gadson,
   Ray Jackson, Al McKay, John Rayford, and Charles Wright)
Drummer: James Gadson
Original Album: *In the Jungle, Babe*
Record Label: Warner Brothers
Recording Date: June, 1969
Recorded at Western Recorders, Hollywood, CA

Historical Overview

Charles Wright & the Watts 103rd Rhythm Street Band was one of the first self-contained funk ensembles
of the late '60s and early '70s. "Love Land" was one of their biggest hits and featured a young man named
James Gadson on drums as well as lead vocals. The song also featured a young rhythm guitar player by the
name of Al McKay. Al later went on to become an important member of one of the most influential bands of
the 1970s, Earth Wind & Fire, and as far as I'm concerned, he was the fire of Earth, Wind & Fire. You should
consider yourself fortunate since you can now play along with him on this play-along CD. He is the featured
guitarist on all of these tracks (except the bonus cuts), and he is the original guitar player on the original
recording of "Love Land."

Approaching the Music

Few drummers on the planet can play the one-handed sixteenth note funk groove like James Gadson because
he just outright *owns* this bad boy. The late legendary studio drummer and member of Toto, Jeff Porcaro,
called Gadson "The Godfather of the sixteenth Note Groove," which, no doubt, is an undisputed fact.
James has a special unorthodox way he approaches the hi-hat on this particular groove. This is a deceivingly
difficult groove to play! Looks so simple doesn't it? It is until you sit down and try to make it flow, especially
at this ridiculously fast tempo. The most important aspect of making this groove come to life is in the hi-hat
approach.

It would benefit you greatly to develop some serious finger and wrist control in order to best achieve the
relaxed state that is necessary to make this groove feel comfortable. Warning: If you don't play this with a real
loose feel you could develop a bad case of tendonitis, so be careful not to tense up. If you do, just stop and
take a break. Don't use your arm to play the groove; instead, use your wrists and fingers.

A good exercise to help develop the speed necessary to master this groove is to use a metronome and try
practicing this exact beat at a tempo that's possible without any strain. It should feel effortless. Don't worry
about how slow the tempo is at first. Just concern yourself with being able to play it smoothly and without
strain. Then, gradually, day by day or week by week, increase the tempo a few beats per minute until you
eventually arrive at this one. It may take some time, perhaps even months, but remember, this is a journey,
not a race. If you suddenly start working out at the gym for the first time, you're not going to be bench-
pressing 250 lbs. at your first workout; you have to build up to it over time with a strategic and calculated
plan. It's the same with mastering certain grooves and tempos on the drums.

My specific approach to this groove is really quite simple: emulate the master himself, case closed. Come to
think of it, that is my approach to everything! Emulate those pioneers who created these grooves. How can
you go wrong when you go to the source?

Recommended Recordings to Help Master This Feel

The Best of Bill Withers: Lean On Me (2000, Sony Music Entertainment)
Charles Wright & The Watts 103rd Street Band's *Express Yourself* (1970, Warner Brothers Records)
Marvin Gaye's *I Want You* (1976, Motown)

10 Classic James Gadson Tracks

1. "Use Me" by Bill Withers, 1972
2. "Dancing Machine" by The Jacksons, 1974
3. "Express Yourself" by Charles Wright & The Watts 103rd Street Rhythm Street Band, 1970
4. "Got To Be Real" by Cheryl Lynn, 1978
5. "I Want You" by Marvin Gaye, 1976
6. "Love Hangover" by Diana Ross, 1976
7. "I Will Survive" by Gloria Gaynor, 1979
8. "Ruby Ruby" by Donald Fagen, 1982
9. "Lonely Town, Lonely Street" by Bill Withers, 1972
10. "Do It Baby" by The Miracles, 1974

(Courtesy of Zoro collection)

James Gadson
The Godfather of groove, chillin' behind a drum kit that has graced countless hit records. I took this picture of him at his house in Los Angeles in 1997. He is sho' 'nuff *Da Man* in my book and, like all the previous drummers featured thus far, another gentle, gracious and humble man!

A rare moment indeed, James Gadson, Steve Gadd, and myself hanging at the Vic Firth booth at the 2007 NAMM show (National Association of Music Merchants) in Anaheim, California. These are two of my favorite drummers and human beings in the world. Quite obviously, the Vic Firth booth is the place to hang and meet legends while soaking in the atmosphere of the groove. Those two guys are a walking encyclopedia of groove and have played on an absolutely tremendous body of great work in American music history!

(Courtesy of Marco Soccolli)

Insight From the Masters

Modern Drummer: "What advice would you have for drummers interested in improving their groove?"
"Understand what it is, and simplify. Most grooves, especially for dance music, are very simple. Even so, to learn them, you have to slow them down. A lot of times we do all these rudimental things to see how fast we can play. I think you have to slow it all down and simplify it. Then you can kind of feel whether it's danceable or not.

"They call it old-school, but that is the school. They want to get that feel, and that's what's missing today. A lot of younger drummers have these great chops, and I love them, but a lot of them don't know about the pocket. They never got to experience it."

—James Gadson
Modern Drummer, September 2007

LOVE LAND

VERSE GROOVE

VERSE GROOVE VARIATION

FILL

PRE-CHORUS FILL

PRE-CHORUS GROOVE

PRE-CHORUS GROOVE VARIATION

OUTRO FILL

JUPITER
TWO-HANDED SIXTEENTH NOTE FEEL

Original Recording Profile

Recording Artist: Earth, Wind & Fire
Producer: Maurice White
Drummer: Freddie White
Original Album: *All 'N All*
Record Label: Columbia
Recording Date: 1977
Recorded at Hollywood Sound, Sunset Sound,
    and Burbank Studios, CA

Historical Overview

This song comes from the Grammy award-winning Earth, Wind & Fire album titled *All 'N All*. The song has a blistering groove that features an incredible horn section, the incomparable vocals of Philip Bailey and Maurice White, a fiery groove from Al McKay on guitar, and, of course, Freddie White on the drums. This type of two-handed sixteenth note groove started showing up on R&B records as early as 1968 with Motown's *Cloud Nine* by The Temptations. Later, in 1971, you heard a similar groove on the title track to the motion picture *Shaft* by Isaac Hayes, featuring Willie Hall on drums. By the mid '70s this groove was flourishing in R&B pop music.

There are two premier funk bands of the 1970s that perfected this feel that quickly come to mind: K.C. and The Sunshine Band with Robert Johnson on drums, and Earth, Wind & Fire featuring Freddie White, Maurice White, and Ralph Johnson sharing the drum chair. This is one of my all-time favorite cuts by EWF, and one of my favorite Freddie White performances. The groove is relentless and proves that good music is good for all time and will always affect people regardless of age or background. My daughter Jordan absolutely loved this groove at the age of five, proving its power to capture all who listen.

Approaching the Music

This groove is all about laying down the sixteenth notes right in the pocket. My focus is to always lock in with the rhythm guitar. Freddie was famous for his economical use of crash cymbals. You will notice that on this groove I rarely hit a crash cymbal on beat 1. Instead, in true Freddie White fashion, I hit the hi-hat on beat 1, leaving it open for the full quarter note value. Freddie was also a drummer of few fills, but when he would do one, it really meant something and had a specific purpose: to enhance the arrangement.

What a concept! It's called being musical. Our goal should be the same, regardless of the particular style of music. Play music, not drums; play for the band, not for yourself; play for the listeners, not other drummers. This unselfish philosophy promotes more of a team spirit, and you will find no better musical example of this than with the drumming of Freddie White and the music of Earth, Wind & Fire!

Recommended Recordings to Help Master This Feel

Earth, Wind & Fire's *All 'N All* (1977, Columbia) and *I Am* (1979, Columbia)
The Best of K.C. and the Sunshine Band (1990, Rhino Records)
The Disco Box (1999, Rhino Records), a 4-CD box set that features 80 songs

10 Classic Freddie White Tracks

1. "I Love You More Than You'll Ever Know" by Donny Hathaway, 1972
2. "Best of My Love" by The Emotions, 1977
3. "Free" by Deniece Williams, 1976
4. "Let's Groove" by Earth, Wind & Fire, 1981
5. "Boogie Wonderland" by Earth, Wind & Fire, 1979
6. "After the Love is Gone" by Earth, Wind & Fire, 1979
7. "Shining Star" by Earth, Wind & Fire, 1975
8. "Serpentine Fire" by Earth, Wind & Fire, 1977
9. "Magic Mind" by Earth, Wind & Fire, 1977
10. "Pride" by Earth, Wind & Fire, 1980

(Courtesy of Zoro collection)

Freddie White

One of the greatest R&B drummers of all time. This man truly played drum parts that fully supported and orchestrated the music of his group. He was a band drummer, not a go-off gladiator. Here Freddie shares some of his magic with me at my home in Southern California back in the late 1990s.

Groove by the bulk! Photographed here are Freddie White and the late great Tony Thompson, hanging out at the NAMM show back in the early 1980s. Two bad dudes who could play a groove like nobody's business! Tony played on legendary cuts with Chic, Sister Sledge, The Power Station, Diana Ross, and a host of others in the '70s and '80s. Together, they represent a whole-lotta groove and a whole-lotta hit songs!

(Courtesy of Zoro collection)

Insight from the Masters

"I'm partial to strong drummers. Most of the drummers I've met who can play strong, can also play very tasty things that are also soft.

"In the studio, I don't use as many cymbals. Sometimes I'll only use one crash and depending on what kind of song, I'll just play it in different places to get different sounds.

"Sometimes, when we're doing demos I'll use a ride cymbal, a crash cymbal, bass drum and snare. If you can be musical with that, then when you have the toms, then you'll know how to use them. If you can take your drums and be musical with them, then you're doing a little bit more that just being a drummer. You're being a musician."

—Freddie White
Modern Drummer, Feb/March 1982

JUPITER

Composed by
LARRY DUNN

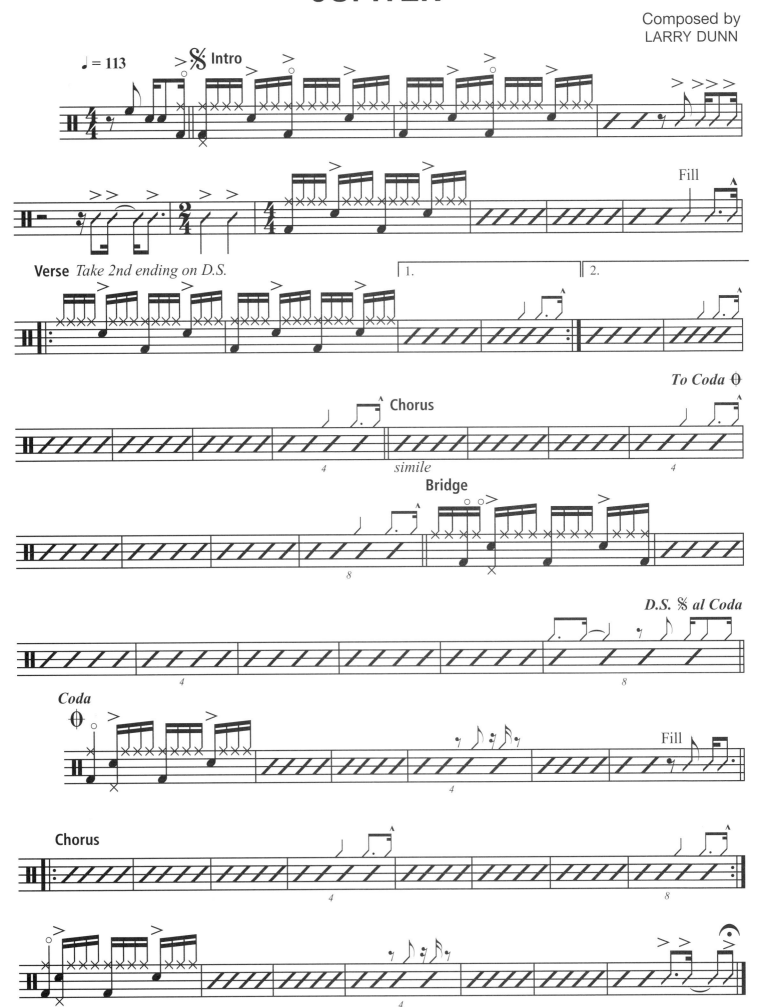

MAIN GROOVE

MAIN GROOVE VARIATIONS

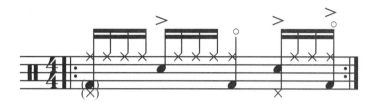

BRIDGE GROOVE

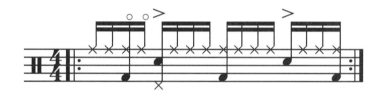

BRIDGE GROOVE VARIATION

CODA GROOVE

CODA GROOVE
MID-PHRASE "HIT"

T.S.O.P.
(THE SOUND OF PHILADELPHIA)
DISCO FEEL

MFSB: LOVE IS THE MESSAGE

Original Recording Profile

Recording Artist: M.F.S.B. featuring The Three Degrees
Producers: Leon Huff and Kenny Gamble
Drummer: Earl Young
Original Album: *Love Is the Message*
Record Label: Philadelphia International
Recording Date: 1973
Recorded at Sigma Sound Studios, Philadelphia, PA

Historical Overview

This song has been the theme for the hit television show *Soul Train* for over 35 years. It was one of the songs that signaled a new direction in R&B music. Intelligent, lush orchestrations, crispy horn arrangements, and a fatback groove by the legendary Earl Young—this was truly great dance music during its finest hour. This rhythm section was the core of Kenny Gamble and Leon Huff's hit—making machinery throughout their heyday. They are featured on numerous hits from the Philadelphia International records label throughout the 1970s, which was their most influential and fertile period. The sound was known as the "Philly soul sound.'"

Approaching the Music

This is straight-up groove, nuttin' but the groove, so help me God, can I get an "Amen" brothers and sisters? It has 1 and 3 on the kick, and 2 and 4 on the snare, with an occasional snare hit on the "ah" of beat two. The thing that makes this groove feel the way it does is the way Earl Young plays his hi-hat. That's where the sweetness lies. He made it feel as smooth as butter, and yet he drove it into the ground. Once again, as with many of the previous feels, the hi-hat approach is the key to the whole groove.

Much of your time should be spent listening intensely to the way all these various great drummers of R&B played time on the hi-hat—that's key. Then a considerable amount of time should be spent specifically emulating each of them.

A lack of revelation in this area is the reason so few drummers make classic R&B music feel authentic and infectious. It's a "feel thang" and I can suggest no better way to get your feel together than by just really respecting what has gone on before and by acknowledging its importance and relevance in your life today. The hi-hat has this mysterious, and yet obvious, power to make people move.

Recommended Recordings to Help Master This Feel

The Philly Sound: Kenny Gamble, Leon Huff and the Story of Brotherly Love 1966–1976 (1997, Epic Legacy)
The Disco Box (1999, Rhino Records), a 4-CD box set that features 80 songs

10 Classic Earl Young Tracks

1. "Bad Luck" by Harold Melvin and The Blue Notes, 1975
2. "Disco Inferno" by The Trammps, 1977
3. "I'll Be Around" by The Spinners, 1972
4. "People Make the World Go Round" by The Stylistics, 1972
5. "Love Train" by The O' Jays, 1973
6. "Back Stabbers" by The O' Jays, 1972
7. "One of a Kind (Love Affair)" by The Spinners, 1973
8. "You Are Everything" by The Stylistics, 1971
9. "Drowning In the Sea of Love" by Joe Simon, 1971
10. "The Rubberband Man" by The Spinners, 1976

(Courtesy of Earl Young)

Earl Young

Inventor of the disco beat, master of the Philly soul sound, and a genuine purveyor of groove! Earl added such musicality and orchestration to every song he played on, and he played on many hits throughout the 1970s. You owe it to yourself to check out his work!

Earl Young pictured here with his group The Tramps who are best remembered for their monstrous 1977 hit "Disco Inferno," featured on the *Saturday Night Fever* soundtrack. This is a photo that Ed signed to me. I had the pleasure of finally meeting him when I played at the Modern Drummer Festival in 2005. At the event. I was given the honor of introducing him to the enthusiastic crowd of drummers that filled the venue.

(Courtesy of Earl Young)

Insight from the Masters

"I loved to play dance music. Ever since listening to James Brown, who was one of my idols, I wanted to play music that people could dance to…. It wasn't so much that I was so great as it was that the three of us had a sound together: bass, drums, and guitar. It's easy to cut a session when you have three guys who know how to work together.….The 'skip beat' was something that I started. The record *Bad Luck* by Harold Melvin has this thing in it where the sock cymbal goes 'shee-ik…shee-ik…shee-ik.'

Nobody else did that before me. They named it disco, but when *Bad Luck* came out, disco wasn't nowhere around. I created the beat with the Spinners. I would play the snare and the tom-tom at the same time, and it would give them a fat sound like the Indians use to have, like BOOM-boom-BOOM-boom-BOOM-boom-BOOM-boom. It worked so well we used it all the time. It gave the Spinners their own sound."

—Earl Young
Modern Drummer, July 1993

T.S.O.P.

Composed by
KENNETH GAMBLE and LEON HUFF

40

CHORUS GROOVE

CHORUS GROOVE VARIATION

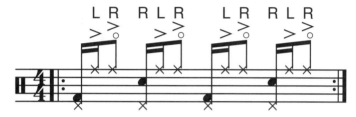

VERSE GROOVE

VERSE GROOVE VARIATION

BRIDGE GROOVE

BRIDGE GROOVE VARIATIONS

BUSTIN' LOOSE
GO-GO FEEL

Original Recording Profile

Recording Artist: Chuck Brown & the Soul Searchers
Producer: James Purdie
Drummer: Ricky Wellman
Original Album: *Bustin' Loose*
Record Label: Source Records
Recording Date: 1979
Recorded at Sigma Sound Studios, Philadelphia, PA

Historical Overview

"Bustin' Loose" was the song that was responsible for bringing go-go music to mainstream America. Prior to this being a national hit in 1979, go-go was a regional style of R&B music that thrived mainly in the Washington D.C., Baltimore, and Virginia areas where it originated. Chuck Brown & the Soul Searchers ruled the go-go scene from the early '70s right through the '80s. Ricky Wellman was the innovative drummer who really personified the go-go beat and helped to define it. He was to go-go what James Brown's drummers were to funk! Daaaaaaaaaa Man!

Approaching the Music

Go-go music is all about playing parts. Each musician's part only makes sense when all the others are playing theirs. Perhaps the single most important aspect of playing this style convincingly is to have complete mastery over the kick drum rhythm. It takes a bit of practice to get the loose swingy feel that comes so naturally to Ricky. The other key component to the kick drum pattern, as well as the more traditional go-go beat, is to have a good understanding of the jazz triplet concept. There are a lot of swung triplets played on the hi-hat on most of the common grooves with the exception of this tune. You absolutely have to pick up some of the recommended recordings listed below to fully understand what I am trying to convey.

Most go-go grooves are a culmination of rhythms that are synonymous with jazz but played with a fat funk backbeat and without much improvisation. Once the beat has begun, the groove is locked up and the key thrown away. Do you remember the fate of the castaways on Gilligan's Island? They never got off the island right? My friends, that should be our approach to this hypnotic trance like groove. You know when you really have the concept down and become a true groove convert? When you loose all desire to leave the island. Forget the mainland bra', the place where chops rule, on the island, groove is God.

Recommended Recordings to Help Master This Feel

Chuck Brown & the Soul Searchers' *Any Other Way To Go?* (1987, Rhythm Attack Recrods)
    This same live recording can be found on the CD titled *Go-Go Swing Live.*
Chuck Brown & the Soul Searchers' *Live '87—D.C. Bumpin' Y'all* (1987)
Trouble Funk Live (1981, Infinite Zero Archives)
Trouble Funk's *Droppin' Bombs: The Definitive Trouble Funk* (1998)

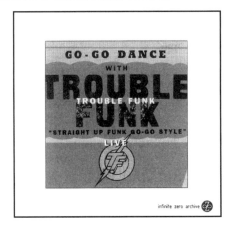

5 Classic Ricky Wellman Tracks

1. "Big Time" by Miles Davis, 1989
2. "Ain't It Funky Now" by Chuck Brown & the Soul Searchers, 1979
3. "Splatch" (live) by Miles Davis, 1998
4. "Hah Man" (*Sinbad* main title song) by Chuck Brown & the Soul Searchers, 1994
5. "A Night In Tunisia" by Chuck Brown & the Soul Searchers, 1994

(Courtesy of Rickey Wellman)

Ricky Wellman

The indisputable master of the go-go groove! Ricky has also lent his truly unique and monstrous groove to Santana and to the legendary Miles Davis. He can be heard on the Miles Davis CDs
In Concert 1988 Parts 1 and 2 and *Time After Time* (1993).

Insight from the Masters

"Not a lot of people are aware of Ricky, but he is a great drummer. He had a lot to do with developing the go-go beat—that street groove created in D.C. that's called hip-hop now. Miles dug that, 'cause go-go is really like a lop-sided swing. The ride is ding-ding-ga-ding, but then you lay that funk beat underneath it, and it swings. So Ricky gave Miles a vehicle to play his own style."

—Joey DeFrancesco
Modern Drummer, September 1997

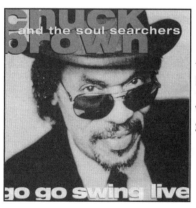

The quintessential live go-go CD from 1986, featuring Ricky Wellman's masterful groove drumming!

Ricky Wellman's drumming is featured on the songs "Jilli" and "Big Time" from the 1989 Miles Davis CD *Amandla*.

BUSTIN' LOOSE

Composed by
CHARLES BROWN

MAIN GROOVE

MAIN GROOVE VARIATIONS

BREAKDOWN VARIATIONS

GROOVE ME
NEW JACK SWING FEEL

Original Recording Profile
Recording Artist: Guy
Drummer: drum machine
Original Album: *Guy*
Record Label: MCA
Recording Date: 1988
Recorded at various studios throughout the New York and
New Jersey area

Historical Overview

This tune set a new precedent when it first hit the airwaves in 1988. It featured this ridiculously funky and utterly infectious groove. The drum beat itself was the main attraction of the song and was deceivingly not as simple as it sounded. This song was produced by Teddy Riley, a pioneer and innovator of a new sound that was dubbed *new jack swing*. New jack swing was a style of R&B music that combined ol' skool soul vocals and harmonies with rap interludes to bring about a fusion of old and new music. It had the swing factor of jazz music with the fat backbeat associated with funk.

The swingy feeling was most often felt in the arena of the drum machine-programmed percussion, bass drum, and hi-hat parts. In essence, the music was swing funk with modern production and recording techniques that made use of one of its newest tools, the drum machine.

Because many of the people that were programming the machines were not drummers themselves, they didn't consider whether any of us mere humans could play the groove in a live situation when called upon to do so later. This put incredible new demands on drummers that were sometimes a bit overwhelming. But if you were willing to stretch the limits of your playing and get out of your comfort zone, this era was a great opportunity to experience new growth.

Approaching the Music

This song is lot more difficult to play authentically than it looks! First off, you have to be able to swing your kick drum quite freely in order to make the drum part flow smoothly. Despite its obvious simplicity on paper, this type of pattern was not commonly played by live drummers of the era, although now a whole generation of R&B drummers play it quite convincingly. Secondly, you have to learn to swing the left hand snare pattern, which is also not very commonplace in a funk type of setting.

The exact pattern that I am playing is a hybrid combination of what the drum machine is doing. The whole point with this tune and many others from this era was for the drummer to emulate the machine as closely as possible. Inevitably, you have to choose to play the most predominant rhythms that are being played by the machine, because it's not possible to play them all. In my case, I chose the clap patterns, snare patterns, and cabasa patterns along with the bass drum. In essence, I built an original groove that is a mixture of all of those parts and therefore came as close as possible to the essence of the feel.

In order for the kick drum to feel as good as the record, you must learn to swing the pattern with a nice range of dynamics. In other words, you can't play the bass drum part at one dynamic level and expect it to feel great. Playing the bass drum at different dynamic levels with varying accent patterns is an extremely complex undertaking. I would suggest that you practice playing accented dotted eighth and sixteenth note patterns on the bass drum to get a real sense of dynamic control. It's just as difficult to get the left hand snare drum parts flowing.

I played the drums live on the set of the DVD shoot and then we later went and re-triggered what I originally played, replacing the live drum sound with sounds that closely match that of the original drum machine on the Guy record. Getting the right drum sounds was a huge part of whether a groove sounded like the era of new jack swing and all other hip-hop oriented drumming.

46

Recommended Recordings to Help Master This Feel

New Jack Hits (1996, Rhino Records)
Guy's *The Future* (1990,MCA Records)

10 Classic Drum Machine Grooves of The Era

1. "777-9311" by The Time, 1982
2. "Perfect Way" by Scritti Politti, 1985
3. "Wanna Be Startin' Somethin'" by Michael Jackson, 1982
4. "Love Light in Flight" by Stevie Wonder, 1984
5. "Everybody Wants to Rule the World" by Tears For Fears, 1985
6. "You Are in My System" by The System, 1983
7. "Candy" by Cameo, 1985
8. "The Way You Make Me Feel" by Michael Jackson, 1987
9. "Poison" by Bell Biv DeVoe, 1990
10. "Part-Time Lover" by Stevie Wonder, 1985

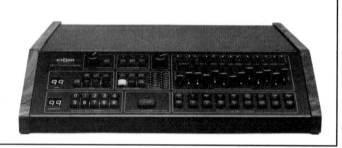

Here is the infamous Linn Drum Machine invented by keyboardist Roger Linn. This culprit caused many drummers to run for cover or to run into the practice room! This was truly one of the most controversial and innovative pieces of machinery in the 1980s and a life-altering bit of technology for all of us who called ourselves drummers. The Linn Drum Machine changed modern drumming and the record industry more than any other rhythmic device of its time.

The incomparable Harvey Mason. His stellar musicianship has been featured on countless records. Seven that I highly recommend are *Breezin'*, *In Flight*, and *Weekend in L.A.* by George Benson; *Mr. Magic* by Grover Washington Jr.; *Chameleon* by Herbie Hancock and the Headhunters; and *Right On Time* and *Looking Out for Number #1* by the Brothers Johnson. He plays every track on all of these CDs and his playing is flawless, inspiring, and invigorating!

(Courtesy of Harvey Mason)

Insight from the Masters

"I work constantly at trying to keep the spacing on the bass drum exactly even. I don't think other people hear it as much as I do, but I have to really think about my bass drum. Your bass drum foot is not like your hands. With your hands, you can really control a lot more spacing between the beats. I fight two constant battles: one is making sure that the bass drum is precise and accurate. Drum machines make you more aware of that because they're really accurate. The other is rather than overplaying, I tend to underplay. I have to be careful not to always play it safe. I always have to make sure I'm thinking fresh."

—Harvey Mason, Studio Legend
Modern Drummer, March 1992

GROOVE ME

Composed by
TEDDY RILEY, TIMOTHY
GATLING, GENE GRIFFIN, and

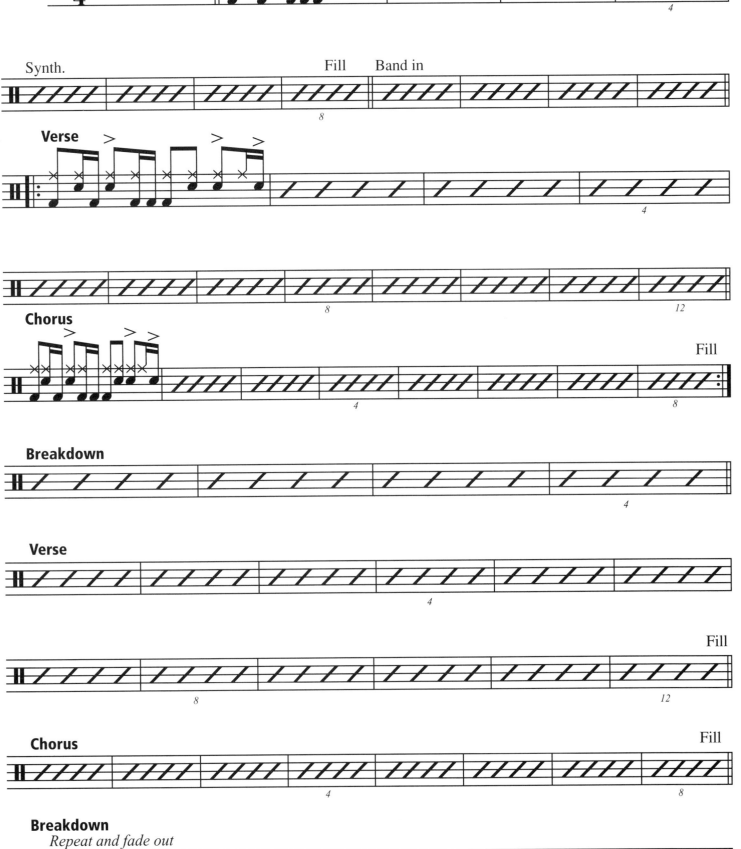

48

MAIN GROOVE

MAIN GROOVE VARIATIONS

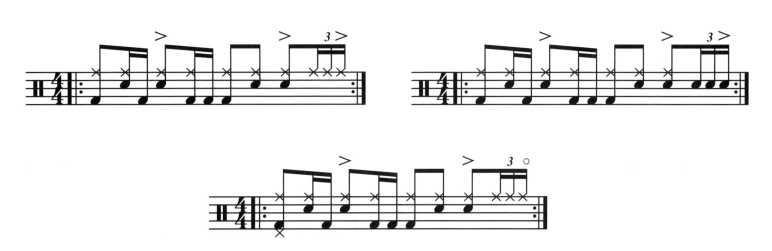

FILLS

YOU
'90s URBAN R&B FEEL

Original Recording Profile

Recording Artist: Janet Jackson
Drummer: Drum machine, loops, and samples
Original Album: *The Velvet Rope*
Record Label: Warner Brothers
Recording Date: 1997

Historical Overview

When this first hit the airwaves, it was one of the funkiest grooves I had heard in a long while. It was a great groove from the nu' skool' of R&B drumming. It has a bit of an ol' skool' vibe mixed with a bit of a modern thing. It's all programmed and uses a combination of drum machines, loops, and samples. This was just a real cutting edge sound at the time. Janet Jackson released this back in 1997 and I thought it would represent the latest in terms of what drum grooves were in that era.

Approaching the Music

The greatest challenge of this groove will be in executing the bass drum pattern and intricate hi-hat pattern with accuracy. Although there is no exact hi-hat pattern on the original recording, my goal was to emulate the shaker pattern as best as I could. On this recording, Russ Miller played the shaker pattern live on a drum pad with a sampled sound as close to the original as possible. Despite the fact that he already had the shaker pattern covered, he happened to add it as an overdub after I recorded the drums live on the set of the DVD shoot. Consequently, I still wanted to play the hi-hat pattern as close to the shaker pattern as possible to get the vibe of the original recording.

If you find you are having difficulty mastering the bass drum pattern and concept I suggest you pick up my book, *The Commandments of R&B Drumming* and turn to page 146 to a section titled "Super Bad Bass Drum Grooves." There I have some very useful single bass drum grooves that, once mastered, will make this groove as smooth as silk. There are some very challenging bass drum patterns written out on pages 147–149 of that book that focus on the concept of mastering thirty second and and sixty fourth note single bass drum patterns, usually a feat left to double bass drums! Also check out my DVD, *The Commandments of R&B Drumming*. I play this song on the DVD and break down the bass drum pattern and applicable exercises in the "House of Z" instructional portion of the DVD.

Recommended Recordings to Help Master This Feel

Janet Jackson's *The Velvet Rope Tour Live In Concert* DVD (1998, Eagle Rock Entertainment)
The Commandments of R&B Drumming DVD by Zoro (2009, Alfred Music Publishing)

A very different Janet Jackson to say the least! I first met Janet backstage at one of my concerts with the New Edition back in 1986 when this shot was taken. Man do we look young or what! Oh yeah…we were!

Insight from the Masters

"I didn't start playing drums until my last year of high school—I was a real late starter—and the teacher made me play bass drum. I worked a lot on my snare rudiments 'cause I really wanted to play snare, as all kids do; nobody wanted to play bass drum. But anyway, I thought he really hated me because I thought that he stuck me with the bass drum like 'OK, you're gonna play the bass drum and all these other guys get to play the snare.'

"But it turns out that he thought I had better time than anybody and he explained to me that the bass drum is a very important instrument and without the bass drum most of the rest of these people can't keep the groove. So he made me feel kind of important by playing the bass drum, even though it was dorky looking. I decided to play it with the attitude, 'OK, cool, I'm gonna keep the groove.' So with drumming, the bass drum has always been my favorite.

"But, you know, I don't play double bass, because I think there's a lot that can be done with single bass. Double bass just ends up being too busy. There's a lot of cats that utilize their double bass incredibly, but I think there's a lot of things you can do groove-wise with the single bass, plus I love playing the hi-hats so much, open and closing things I can't do that with the double basses. Most of the music I play it's just a real groove thing, laying the pocket two and four or whatever the groove happens to be."

—Zoro

Rhythm magazine, September 1989

51

YOU

Composed by
JANET JACKSON, JAMES HARRIS III, TERRY LEWIS, ALLEN SYLVESTER, HAROLD BROWN, MORRIS DEWAYNE DICKERSON, LEROY L. JORDAN, CHARLES MILLER, OSKAR LEE, and HOWARD E. SCOTT

♪ = 142

Intro

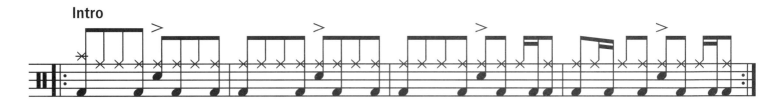

Verse
simile

Pre Chorus
Repeat 3 times

Chorus

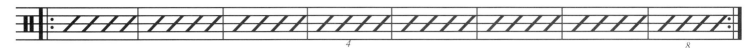

Verse

Pre Chorus

Chorus
Repeat 4 times

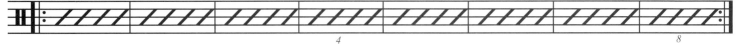

Breakdown
Repeat and fade

MAIN GROOVE

MAIN GROOVE VARIATIONS

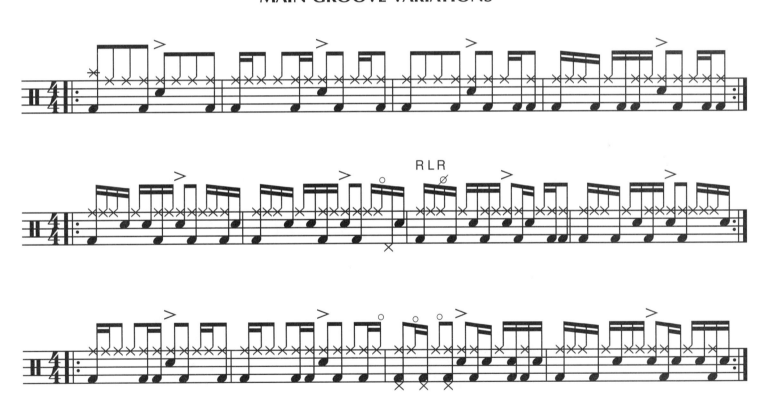

SHO 'NUFF
EIGHTH NOTE FUNK FEEL

Original Recording Profile

Recording Artist: Zoro
Producers: Zoro, Robby Robinson
Drummer: Zoro
Original Album: *The Commandments of R&B Drumming* Book and CD
Publisher: Alfred Music Publishing (2007)

Historical Overview

This tune was co-written with some of my touring colleagues Rex Robinson, Robby Robinson, and Fino Roverato. We came up with this groove at a soundcheck and recorded most of the basic rhythm tracks right on stage with ADAT machines, which were the hip machines of the day. We recorded everything except the drums, and some overdubs on keyboards, which were done later in Los Angeles.

Approaching the Music

The vibe that I was after with this tune was just some straight-up later-'70s funk, à la the Gap Band, Con Funk Shun, Slave, Roger and Zapp, and a plethora of other R&B groups that defined the sound of the era. This is just a groove with a few section changes, really fairly simple.

Recommended Recordings to Help Master This Feel

Phat Trax Series, Vol. 1–7 (1994, Rhino Records)

(Courtesy of Josh D'Aubin)

Chillin' at home with my red sparkle DW kit and my Sabian HHX Groove cymbals. My set up is a constant source of joy and inspiration. It always stirs my creativity, inspires me to practice, and draws out my best performance. I sincerely appreciate the creative geniuses who dream up and manufacture the gear that I am fortunate enough to play. Without a doubt, a great instrument inspires a great performance and I am grateful for mine.

Here I am standing in front of the Vic Firth booth at the NAMM show for the release of my signature stick. I have been with Vic Firth for over 25 years and played their sticks throughout my entire career, so it's a real honor to have a signature stick with them. This was really cool for my kids to see me larger than life. Now maybe they'll listen to me when I tell them to take out the trash?

Steve Gadd and I both toured with famous French artists throughout France in 1993. Here we are at one of our mutual concert dates we played. When you're out of the country for months, it's sure good to run into friends from back home, especially when he is one of the coolest guys in the world and one of the greatest musicians on the planet!

Insight from the Masters

"I mean, creativity isn't just coming up with a tricky drum part. Creativity is creating music with a bunch of people that you're playing with. It's not a real personal thing: you're part of a unit, creating a product that's going to be sold, for an artist who's written the stuff. You have to work together to come out with music…

"But then, after I started getting into the studios, I saw the challenge of a simpler way of playing. I'm not saying I threw that other way of playing out the window. That's still valid and that approach might be good in certain situations. But there are other, more laid-back approaches that are just as good too.

"You can take the opposite end—playing the simplest, littlest amount you can play—and find that challenge. It's just two different approaches. It's not always what you do on the drums that's noticed. It's what you don't do, a lot of times, that's noticed. When you're first starting out, and you've got a space to play, you might be confused about what is going to impress people.

"Even though you've got a space there, where you can play some drums and really razzle-dazzle them technically, sometimes that will be less impressive than if you sort of let that space go by an play a real simple little thing. It's better for the music. I think that a good rule is to always think in terms of music first, and let that determine how complicated the fill is or how loud it is.

"And then eventually I was able to channel that energy into an enthusiasm for the music, and sort of separate myself from the drums, personally, I was able to channel it and start playing less. You start realizing that when you put that much energy into it, you might be on the upper side of the time. You just have to think about the other way to do it. I think the only way to find out about playing on top is to put a click on and then play loud and soft with it. If you can understand that it's real natural to get on top when you're playing loud, then you can start to understand it."

—Steve Gadd, studio legend
Modern Drummer, July 1983

SHO 'NUFF

Composed by
ZORO and
ROBBY ROBINSON

VERSE GROOVE

VERSE GROOVE VARIATION

CHORUS GROOVE

CHORUS GROOVE VARIATION

BRIDGE

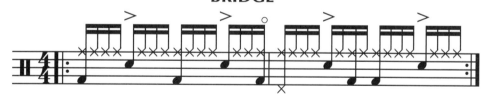

FILL

SOLI VARIATIONS

SOULEDIFIED
ONE HANDED SIXTEENTH NOTE FEEL

Original Recording Profile

Recording Artist: Zoro
Producers: Zoro, Russ Miller, and Robby Robinson
Drummer: Zoro
Original Appearance: *The Commandments of R&B Drumming* Book and CD
Publisher: Alfred Music Publishing (2007)

Historical Overview

I wrote this song with my partner Robby Robinson for my book and CD, *The Commandments of R&B Drumming*. The inspiration for this song came from my deep love for the one hand sixteenth note groove, à la Charles Wright & The Watts 103rd Street Rhythm Band, Rufus, Earth, Wind & Fire, and Barry White. This feel is one of the most predominant grooves of the '70s R&B scene and is still alive and well today. It's a staple pop feel every drummer needs to have a handle on. Believe it or not, this is one of the hardest grooves to own with authenticity.

Approaching the Music

My approach to playing this feel was to play the way James Gadson would have played it. There is a nice little drum break where I get a chance to get a little funky with it. On the drum breakdown there are a couple of things that I do that might be hard to figure out just from listening to this CD. So much of drumming remains a mystery until you can see what the drummer is actually playing, at least it has always been that way for me.

If you don't already have my DVD *The Commandments of R&B Drumming*, you may want to consider picking it up. It makes coping these grooves a lot easier. I introduce a few of my favorite drumming concepts in this tune and in the breakdown. One of them is the use of unison sixteenth notes played by both the hi-hat and snare drum and adding to that some very syncopated bass drum patterns. I do this only occasionally to spice up the groove and for very short increments of time, so as not to get too busy.

The other is perhaps my favorite way to elevate the excitement level of a bridge or any section of a tune where you want to give it a slightly different feel and texture. It's a crossover pattern between the hi-hat and ride cymbal. This is all done with one hand: you play all the eighths on the hi-hat on the downbeats and the "&"s, and all the "e"s and "ah"s on the ride cymbal. It's kind of tricky at first, and it takes some serious coordination to pull it off smoothly, but it's a real sweet way of lifting the groove somewhat without being too busy. The key to pulling this off at this tempo is not to have your ride too far away, because the further it is, the harder it is to play in time because it's happening so fast.

I also employ the use of thiry second and sixty fourth notes on the bass drum within the groove itself. The key is to use them sparingly and to drop them in at the funkiest rhythmic point possible. This concept is a fairly difficult one. For more information on this, please refer to what I previously mentioned about bass drum pointers in the "approaching the music" section on page 50. The same thing applies here.

Recommended Recordings to Help Master This Feel

The Ohio Players' *Honey* (1975, Mercury) Check out the song "Fopp" and drummer James Diamond Williams for some fancy bass drum work along these lines. This is really where this stuff came from!
The Commandments of R&B Drumming DVD by Zoro (2002, Alfred Music Publishing)

(Courtesy of Zoro collection)

Here I am playing behind Lenny Kravitz. This night we played with the legendary James Brown in New York City at a special concert event for *Rolling Stone* magazine.

Insight from the Masters

Modern Drummer: "You have an incredibly fast bass drum foot. You're able to duplicate some of the contemporary patterns-created by machine-that feature a straight 2 and 4 backbeat with fast 16th notes on the bass drum. How did you develop that?"

Zoro: "Well, the desire to do that came from the fact that most drummers felt that those "machine-made" bass drum patterns were impossible to play. I've always told myself that, the first time you say you can't do something, you won't be able to do it.

"I always thought it was possible. I was pretty lucky in that I do have a fairly fast foot naturally, but then I worked on it a lot. I would work with a Linn Drum machine, programming a lot of those weird 'street beats.' And then I'd try to play them live. I'd start them off at a slow tempo and try to pick apart the groove that I had made up-which would be real funky and complicated. I had practiced out of books for years, and I finally wanted to practice something based on my own concept. I decided to be the first drummer who could play like a drum machine but with feeling."

—Zoro
Modern Drummer, February 1986

SOULEDIFIED

Composed by
ZORO and
ROBBY ROBINSON

60

CHORUS GROOVE

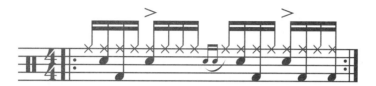

CHORUS GROOVE VARIATION

VERSE GROOVE

VERSE GROOVE VARIATION

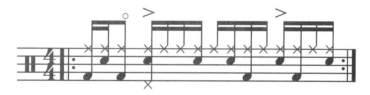

MID-CHORUS "HITS"

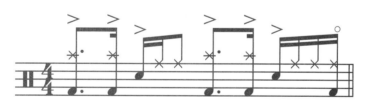

SOLI LICKS

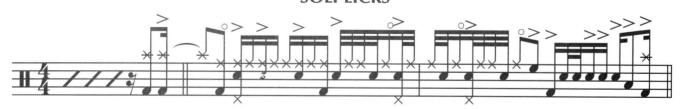

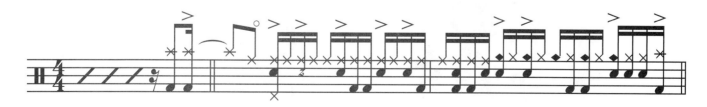

THE FUNKY MONK
HIP-HOP SWING FEEL

Original Recording Profile

Recording Artist: Zoro
Producers: Zoro and Robby Robinson
Drummer: Zoro
Original Album: *Zoro the Funky Drummer*
Record Label: Z-Force Music

Historical Overview

This is yet another song that I wrote with my partner Robby Robinson while we were on the road with Frankie Valli & the Four Seasons. We were in the middle of nowhere for a week, so I thought this would be a great place to do some writing. I wanted something with a hip-hoppy, new jack swingish feel, but with some hipper chords that you might hear in more of a jazz or fusion setting. We actually recorded the basic tracks including saxophone in my hotel room at the Hyatt Regency in downtown Columbus, Ohio a few weeks later. Then, when we got back to Los Angeles, I recorded the drums in the studio. The original drum track appeared on the CD portion of my book, *The Commandments of R&B Drumming*. This drum track is the second version that was recorded live on the set of the DVD shoot.

Approaching the Music

My approach to this tune was to combine the stylistic elements of a new jack swing groove (the swingy left handed snare patterns, complete with ghost notes and an occasional buzz) with a bit of a go-go groove (the bass drum pattern) and put a phat backbeat on it. I wanted to do something exciting with the hi-hats in the B section without taking away too much from the groove so I came up with this sixteenth note triplet thing between the left hand and the hi-hat. This is simpler than it sounds and looks. All I really did was play eighth notes with the hi-hat foot and played the last two partials of the triplet with my left hand on the hi-hat. But the key is to close the hi-hat immediately after the last partial of the triplet and make it real clean. The right hand is then free to play the backbeat with some occasional ghosting.

For a visual representation of this groove, pick up my DVD *The Commandments of R&B Drumming*. I break down all the details in the DVD and break down the hi-hat part real slowly. I really enjoyed playing this tune. By the way, the drum track was played completely live on the set of the DVD shoot, but later Russ Miller went into his studio and retriggered the kick and snare through his computer with some more hip-hop oriented sounds. If you already own my first book, you will hear a noticeable difference in the way the drums sound.

Recommended Recordings to Help Master This Feel

Stolen Moments: Red, Hot & Cool (1994, GRP)
Guru Jazzmatazz Volume 1 (1993, Chyrsalis)

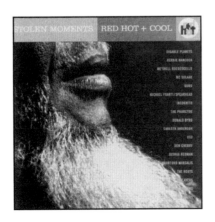

Here I am pounding the skins behind Lenny Kravitz and having a blast as I always did. This photo was taken in Switzerland during one of our many European tours throughout the years.

Steve Gadd and I hanging again for an autograph signing at the Vic Firth booth at the 2007 NAMM show in Anaheim, California. I first met Steve back in 1985 when he was kind enough to invite me to one of his New York recording sessions. It was unreal! Then he topped that off by coming with his wife Carol to see me play at Madison Square Garden with the New Edition in the same year. It was a thrill for me to have Steve at my show and one of the experiences that I will always cherish. The Gadds have always been so very kind and encouraging to me.

Insight from the Masters

"Playing good time is very important, whether it's slow time, or hardly playing anything sometimes and leaving space. Put the bass drum on the back beat and on the money for five or ten minutes and try to keep it steady. I could be playing for a month and never run into anything that requires a lot of technique. It might require that I play very simply. If you've got a lot of chops and you get bugged because the music doesn't require great chops, it's difficult to be open minded about the music.

"You have to get beyond that wall you set up for yourself. You have to see the truth in the simpler ways of playing. That was a real challenge to me. I realized that technique doesn't mean a shit if you can't play a back beat in a place that fits, and lock it in. I had never thought about that before, mainly because I didn't grow up playing rock. I grew up playing bop. I heard kids who didn't have my technique but they could lay down a back beat that would kick ass. I started practicing playing uncomplicated things and solid time. To play as simply and as unnoticed as I could became as challenging as playing at a high energy level. They're still both equally challenging to me."

—Steve Gadd
Modern Drummer, October 1978

"When I'm learning a new song I rarely sit behind a drum kit. I just really listen to a song very closely and try to focus on all the different parts and transitions. I listen to all instruments and individually so I know what the other guys are doing and I really listen to the feel and the groove and the sound of the drums. If I just put on a disc and start playing to it I somehow never really learn the structure or the feel. Usually, I'll end up jamming to the original drum part instead of playing the part itself. By just listening it's much easier to really get into the drum part."

—Zoro
Drummer, February 2005

FUNKY MONK

Composed by
ZORO and
ROBBY ROBINSON

VERSE GROOVE

VERSE GROOVE VARIATIONS

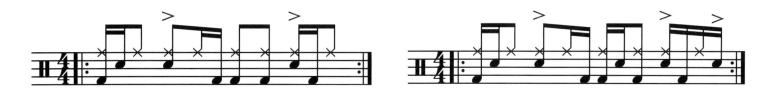

CHORUS GROOVE

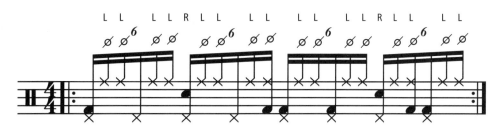

CHORUS GROOVE VARIATION

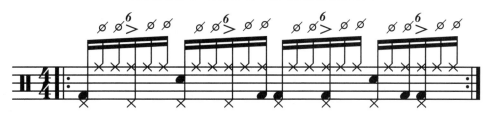

SOLO GROOVE VARIATION

The Greatest Groove Ever Told!

In the beginning, there was the groove, and the groove was with God. And the groove was God. Then God made man and liked what he had made. But God looked down upon man and saw that it was not good for man to be alone. So in His loving kindness, God gave to man a taste of heaven on Earth. He gave to him the groove, that cosmic force that actually holds the universe in place. So man was no longer alone, and since then has experienced unspeakable joy from this invisible friend we call the groove, the beat, the pulse, the pocket.

And God, being just and fair, saw to it that all of mankind could equally experience the divine magical powers and hypnotic effects of the groove. Both musician and audience would benefit from the therapeutic wonders of the groove. But being a God of purpose, He gave to all mankind free will and the ability to choose, and since then one question has always remained: To groove or not to groove? That is the question. It is His will that no man perish from a lack of groove, for His greatest desire is for us to choose to groove, but He cannot force us to make that choice.

And remember, it was foretold that man could not live by bread alone, but by each and every groove to cometh forth from the heavenly realms. So groove on, brothers and sisters, with all your heart, soul, might, and strength, and therefore glorify your God! God's gift to us is the groove; our gift to Him is how we develop it and serve others with it. So surrender to the almighty groove, for only then will you be truly free!

Psalm 150: 5
"Praise Him with resounding cymbals; praise Him with loud clashing cymbals!"

The Minister of Groove

Zoro's Ten Commandments of Groove

He who abides by these Ten Commandments will be the greatest in the kingdom of groove! He who does not, surely will not gig!

I · Thou shalt serve the creator of the groove.

II · Thou shalt humble thyself and become a servant of the groove.

III · Thou shalt place no other instruments before the drums.

IV · Thou shalt serve the music and not thyself.

V · Thou shalt not covet thy brother's chops; instead, covet his groove.

VI · Thou shalt play from thy heart and not from thy head.

VII · Thou shalt honor and respect the forefathers of the groove.

VIII · Thou shalt offer thyself up as a living sacrifice to the groove.

IX · Thou shalt use thy spirit of creativity to innovate the groove.

X · Thou shalt impart the wisdom of the groove to the next generation.